ELECTRIC
MAZES

ELECTRIC MAZES

Juliet & Charles Snape

Julia MacRae Books

LONDON SYDNEY AUCKLAND JOHANNESBURG

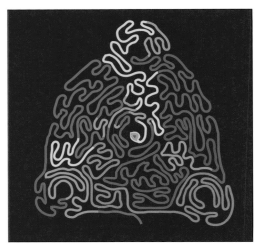

TROYTOWN

First published 1999

©1999 Juliet & Charles Snape
1 3 5 7 9 10 8 6 4 2
Juliet and Charles Snape have asserted their rights under
the Copyright,
Designs and Patents Act l988 to be identified as author
and illustrator of this work.
First published in the United Kingdom in 1999 by
Julia MacRae,
Random House, 20 Vauxhall Bridge Road, London SWlV 2SA
Random House UK Limited Reg No 954009
A CIP catalogue record for this title is available from
the British Library

ISBN 1 85681 624 9

Printed in Hong Kong

INTRODUCTION

Complicated pathways have always fascinated people, from the Greek legend of the minotaur in an underground labyrinth to new three-level hedge mazes with bridges and tunnels.

LABYRINTH DESIGN

Sometimes mazes have been created with mystical objectives, such as ones drawn outside doorways to ward off evil spirits and ghosts; sometimes the motive is obscure, such as in mizmazes, and sometimes they are purely recreational, as at Hampton Court or the mirror mazes at a fair ground. They are also used to test intelligence and learning behaviour in animals and robots.

This collection of mazes was created electronically. Visually exciting, they will test your skill and challenge your wits! Not always marked with Starts and Finishes, the puzzle can be where to enter the maze and where to come out. There are intersections to cross, arrows to follow and multi-coloured paths to find. Solutions are supplied at the end of the book for you to check your route is correct!

Find a route along the multicoloured paths and through the blac

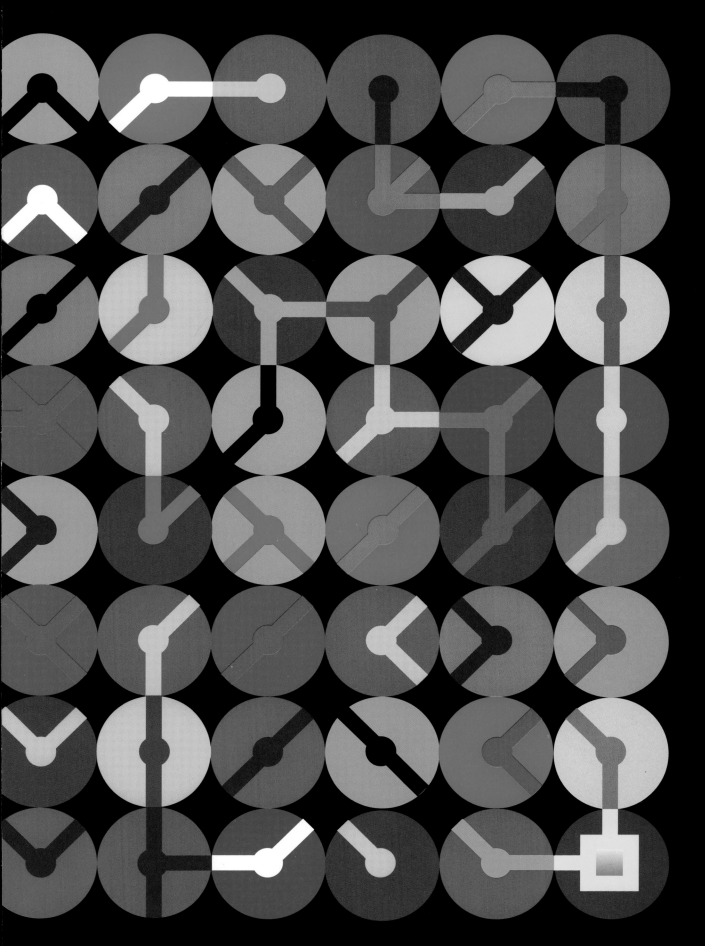

intersections. Start in the circle at the top left and finish in the square at the bottom right.

HEDGE MAZE

This maze is based on the hedge maze
found at Hampton Court Palace.
Enter at the top and find a way
to the centre.

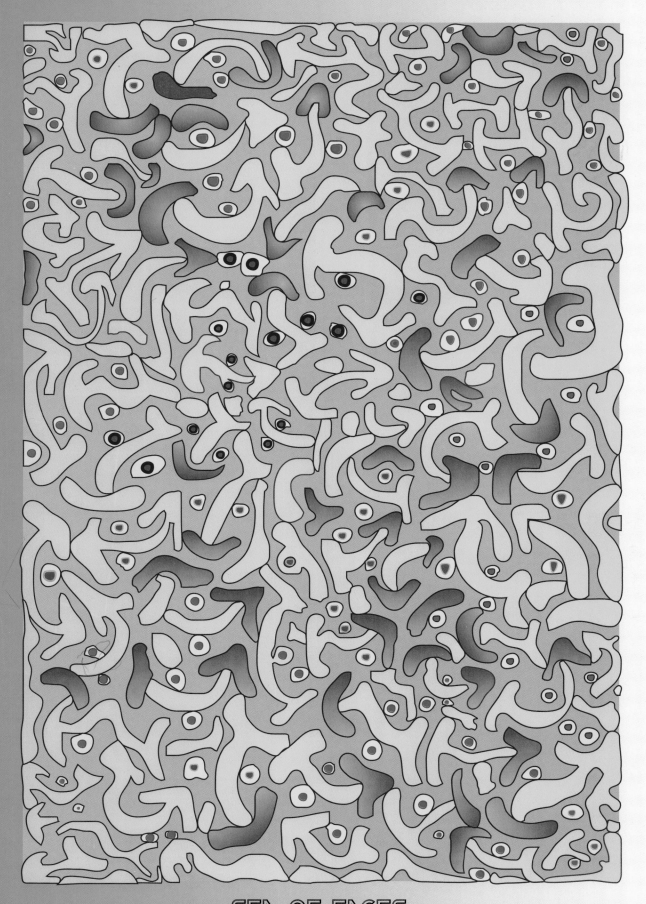

SEA OF FACES

Enter the blue sea on the left side.
Find a way around the maze of faces to exit on the right.

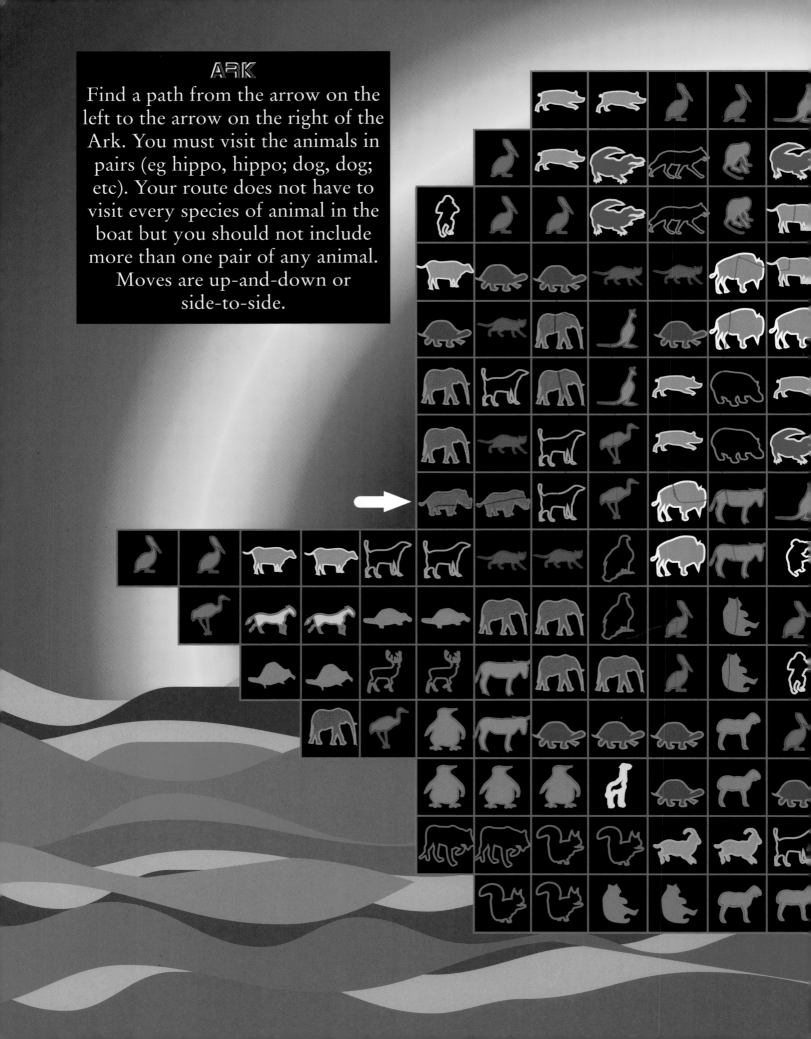

ARK

Find a path from the arrow on the left to the arrow on the right of the Ark. You must visit the animals in pairs (eg hippo, hippo; dog, dog; etc). Your route does not have to visit every species of animal in the boat but you should not include more than one pair of any animal. Moves are up-and-down or side-to-side.

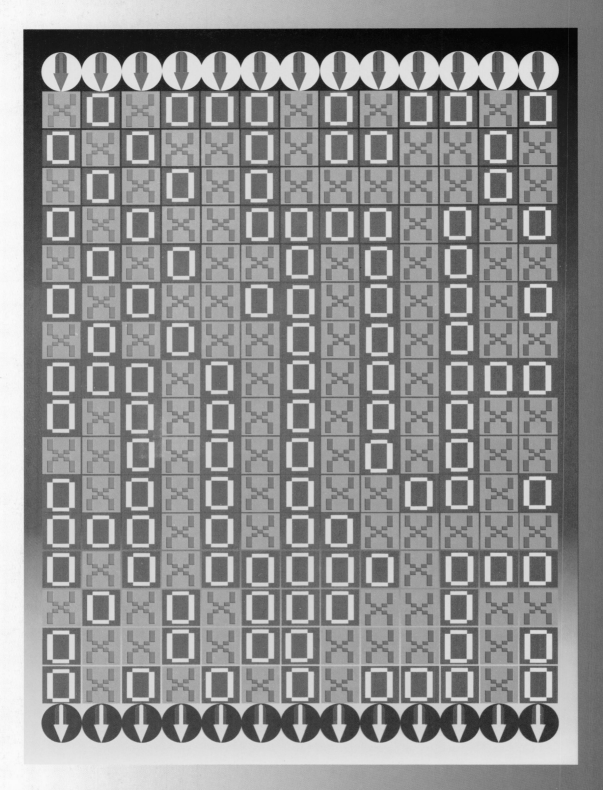

NOUGHTS AND CROSSES
Following either OXOX... or XOXO...
Find a route from one of the letters in the top row to one
of the letters in the bottom row.
Finish on either letter (O or X) so long as it is in sequence.
You may only move up-and-down or from
side-to-side, no diagonals.

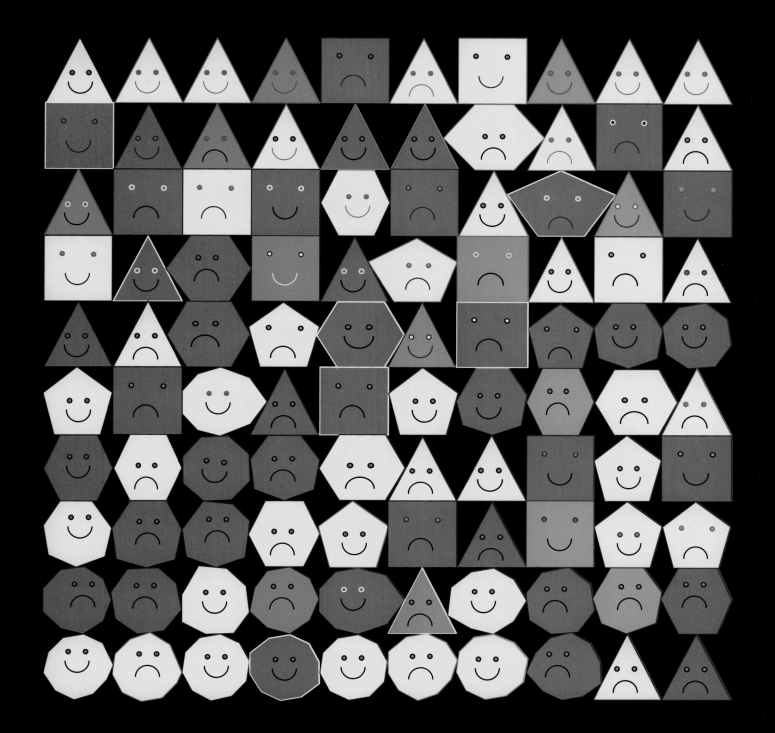

THREE IN ONE

There are **three** different ways through this maze. Each way only allows horizontal and vertical moves. Each route starts on one of the shapes in the top row and finishes on one in the bottom row.

Route l: Yellow, red, yellow, red, yellow...
Route 2: Alternately happy, sad; happy, sad...
Route 3: Increasing number of sides, △(3); △,□,(3,4); △,□,⬠(3,4,5); ...◯(...10). Each time you begin a count start with a triangle.

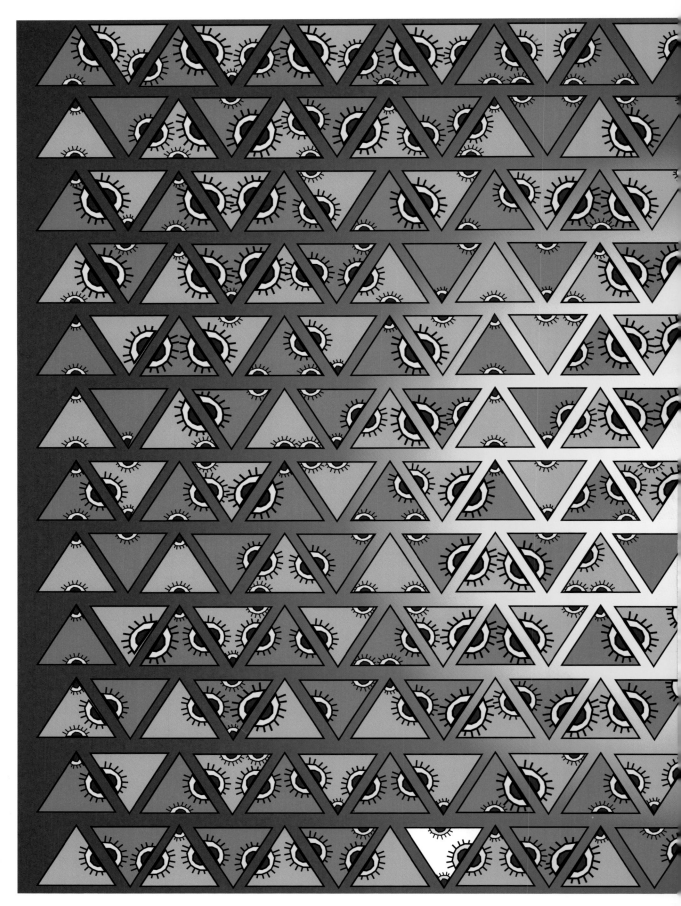

EYE TO EYE   Start on the blue triangle at the top of the maze and finish on the
by making eye-to-eye contact. Your route might go up, down or

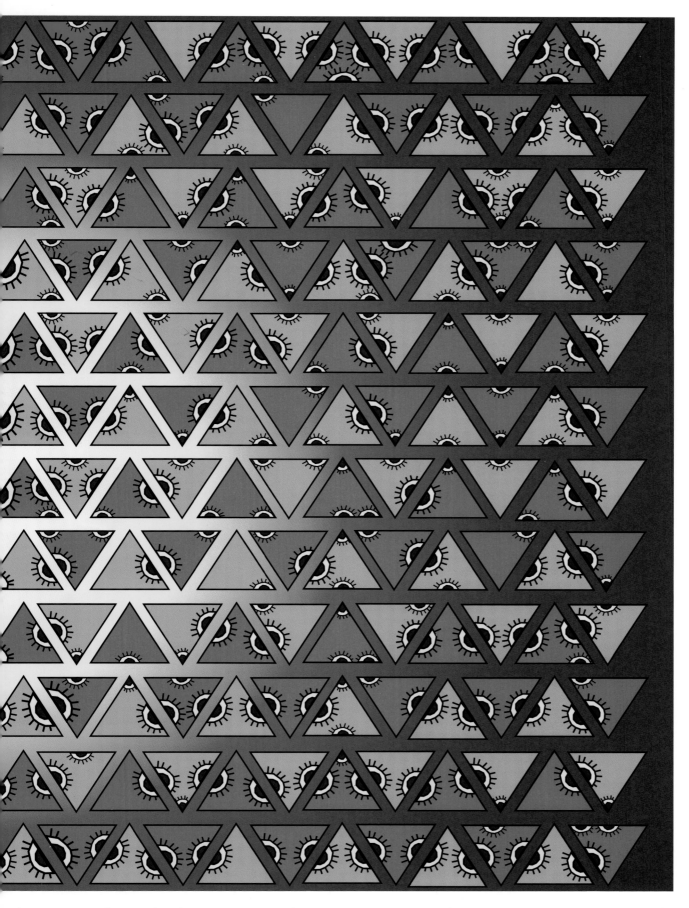

white triangle at the bottom. Find a route jumping from one triangle to another
diagonally… but one eye must be looking directly at another.

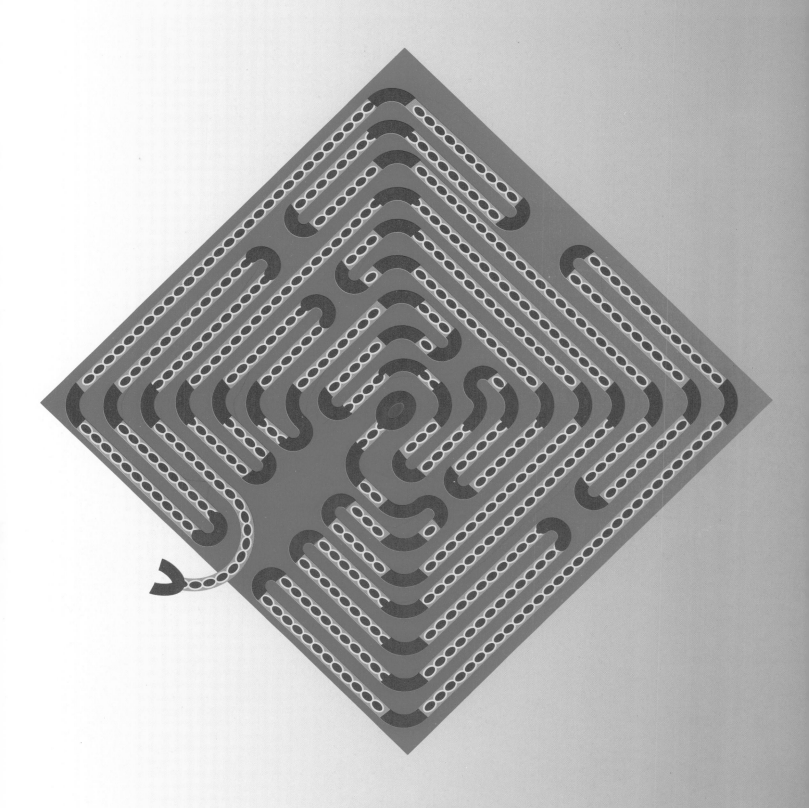

MIZMAZE

Mizmazes were cut into hillsides during the
Middle Ages. Their purpose is unknown.
Follow the path of the snake from tail
to head.

TRIANGLES

Start at shape one and find a pathway between the triangles
to take you through the other numbered shapes in order.
You may travel through the numbered shapes but not the
triangles. You should not retrace any part of your path or
cross an earlier one.

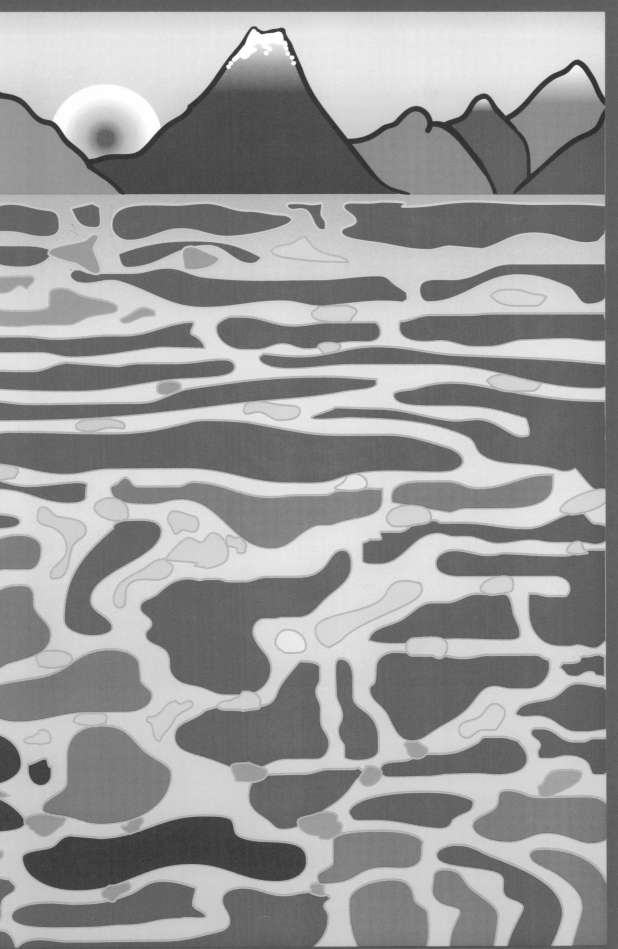

THROUGH THE LAKE

Find a way along the watery paths from the outside of the lake to reach the golden carp.

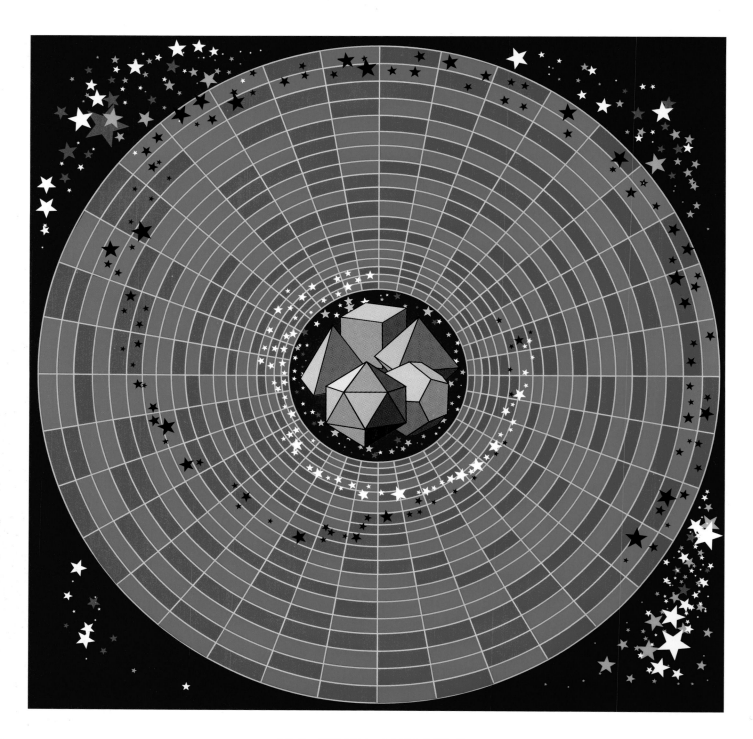

TO THE CENTRE

Starting from a block on the outside ring,
find a path to the centre.
Your route must follow a pattern:

red, blue, red, blue… or blue, red, blue, red…

Only side-to-side and up-and-down moves are
allowed – no diagonals. The stars are merely
to mislead you!

WHICH ONE?

Start at any of the circles on the edge of the maze.
Which path will take you to the centre?

CIRCLE-TO-CIRCLE

You cannot cross a shape which has a square at its centre. Find a route from the top to the bottom moving diagonally only.

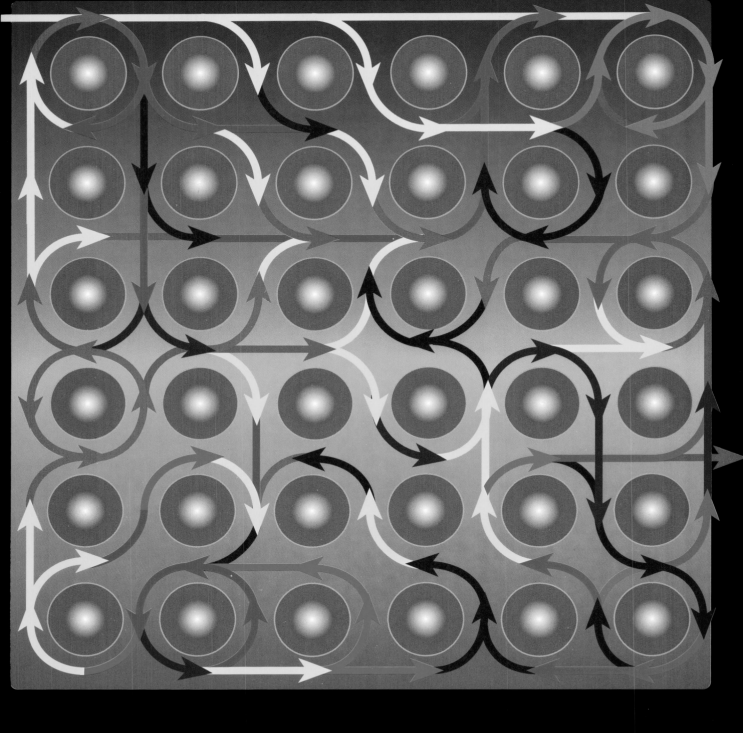

ONE WAY
Start in the top left corner.
Follow the different coloured arrows to find

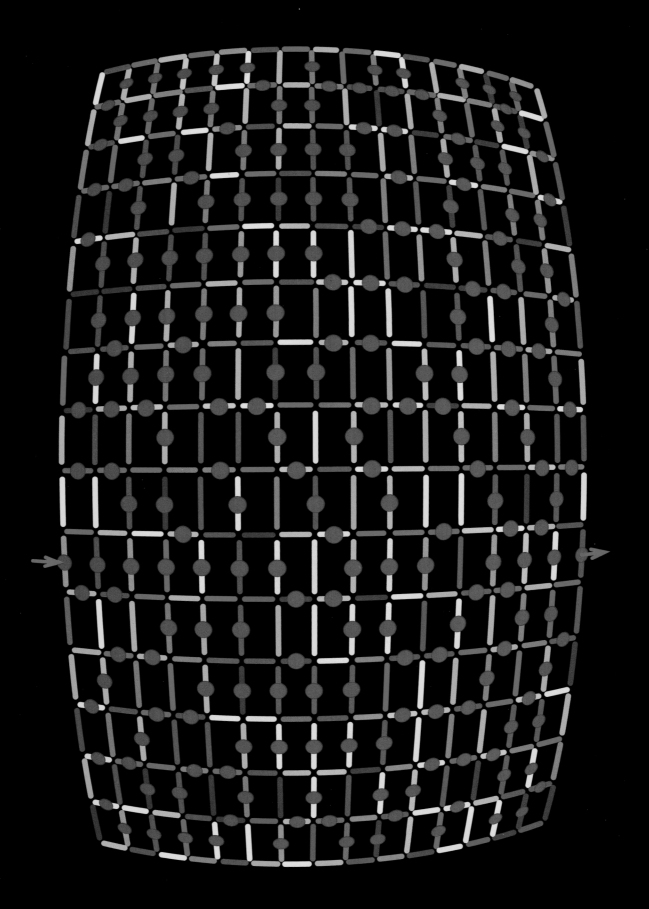

CURVED

Start at the arrow on the left. Move from room to room only through the magenta circles. Reach the exit on the other side.

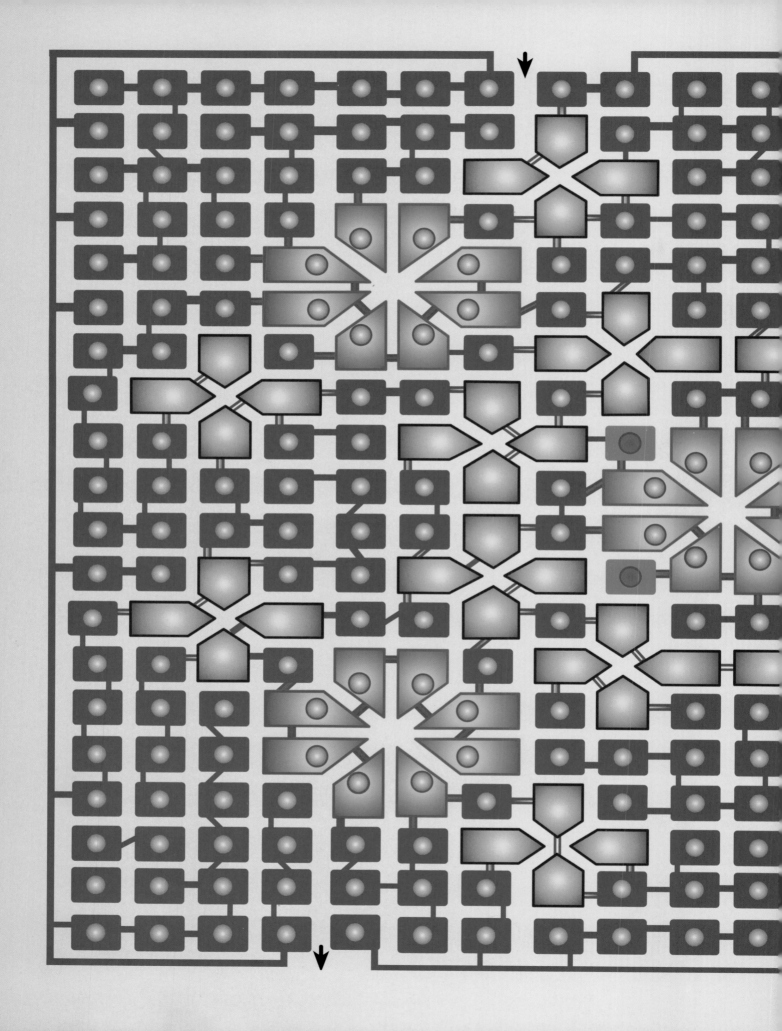

CHINESE PATHWAYS
Start at the entrance and find a route along the pathways to exit.

SOLUTIONS

Following are the solutions. In some of the mazes there are short alternate loops, where they exist they are shown as a broken line. No solution is given to Mizmaze.

DISK WAYS

SEA OF FACES

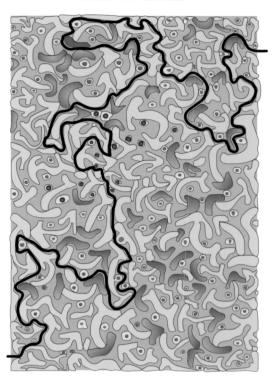

HEDGE MAZE

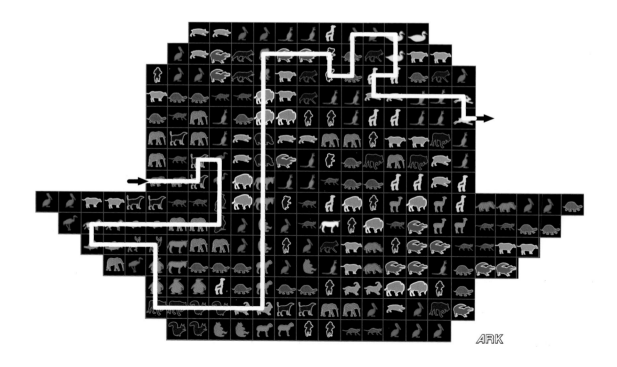

ARK

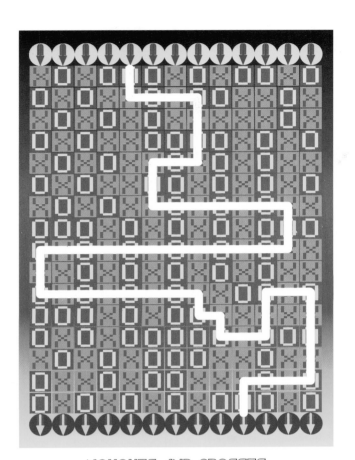

NOUGHTS AND CROSSES

ROUTE 2   ROUTE 3   ROUTE 1

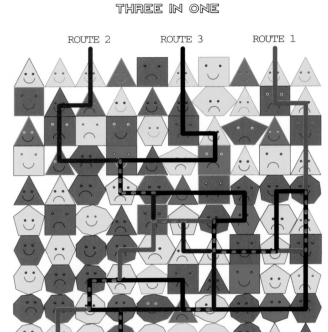

EYE TO EYE

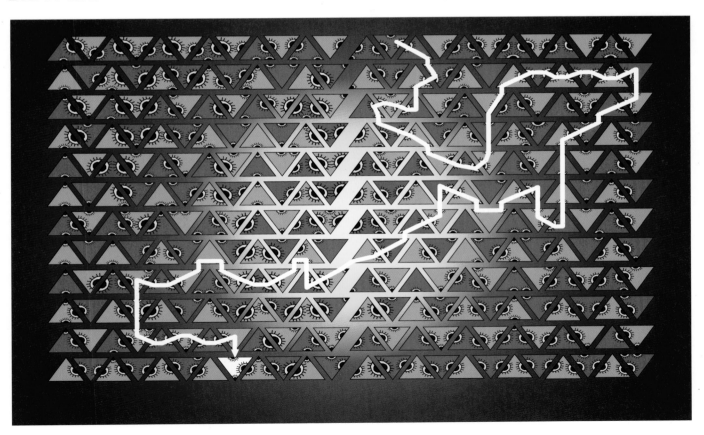

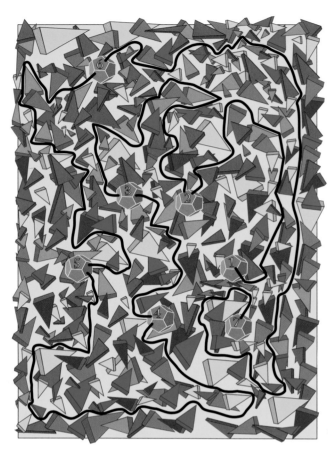

TRIANGLES

THROUGH THE LAKE

TO THE CENTRE

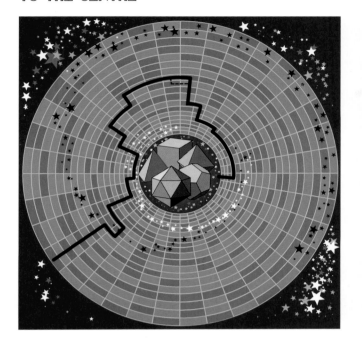

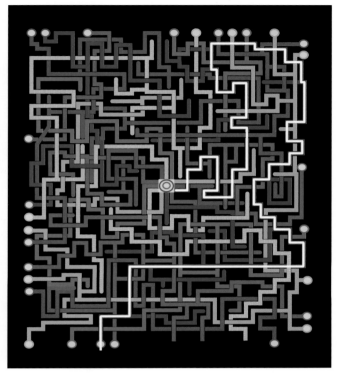

WHICH ONE?

CIRCLE-TO-CIRCLE

ONE WAY

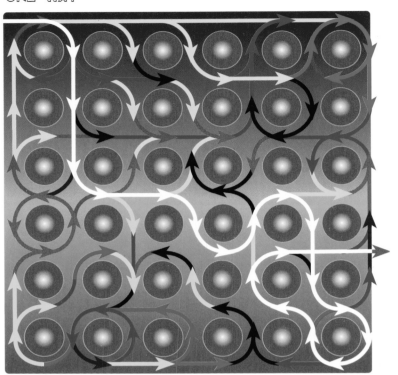

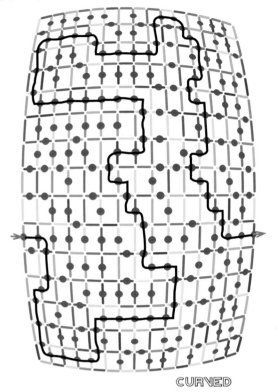

CURVED

CHINESE PATHWAYS

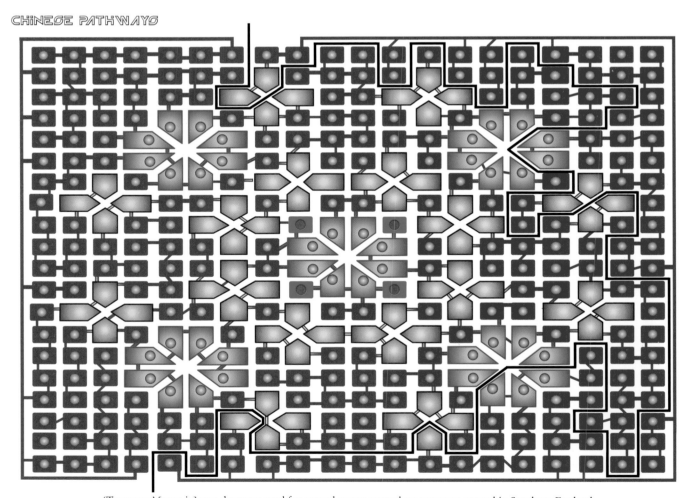

'Troytown' [page iv] was the name used for several mazes created on common ground in Southern England
in the 17th and early 18th centuries; we know of these from written accounts.

'Labyrinth Design' [page v]. Maze designs like this have been found on coins around Knossos, Crete, home of the Minotaur.